Original title:
Love's Learning Lab

Copyright © 2024 Swan Charm
All rights reserved.

Author: Sabrina Sarvik
ISBN HARDBACK: 978-9916-86-623-8
ISBN PAPERBACK: 978-9916-86-624-5
ISBN EBOOK: 978-9916-86-625-2

## The Compass of Compassion

In the heart of the silent night,
Whispers of kindness take their flight.
With each step in love's soft embrace,
We gather strength, we find our place.

A compass turns, the needle glows,
Guiding us where the warm wind blows.
Through valleys deep and mountains tall,
Compassion's call unites us all.

In every smile, in every tear,
Compassion's voice is always near.
It mends the wounds of those who fall,
A gentle touch can heal us all.

Through stormy skies and skies so clear,
We hold each other, year to year.
The world reflects what we can share,
A bond of love beyond compare.

So let your heart be wide and free,
A compass true to lead you and me.
In the journey we always find,
Compassion's grace, eternally kind.

## **The Science of Togetherness**

In atoms we collide, energies align,
Defying all the odds, our love's design.
With every pulse and beat, a force unfolds,
Together stronger, a bond that never folds.

From stardust we emerged, a cosmic dance,
In harmony we live, embracing chance.
The universe conspired, our paths entwined,
In this grand experiment, love redefined.

## Affectionate Insights

In gentle whispers, secrets softly shared,
A glance, a smile, knowing someone cared.
In the warmth of touch, we find our bliss,
Each moment cherished, in a lover's kiss.

Through trials faced, a bond that's fortified,
In storms we weather, we're side by side.
With every heartbeat, our truths laid bare,
Affection breeds strength, a love to declare.

## The Milestones of Us

Footprints on the path, marking where we've been,
Each laugh, each tear, where love has always been.
From dreams we started, to plans now unfold,
In chapters we write, our journey is told.

Through quiet moments, our memories grow,
The milestones reached, in love's gentle flow.
With hands intertwined, we face what's ahead,
Together, always, in the words we've said.

## Chronicles of Connection

In stories shared, we weave a tapestry,
Of laughter and tears, a shared symphony.
With each turning page, new adventures arise,
In the heart of the tale, we find our skies.

This chronicle unfolds, through time and space,
In each fleeting moment, we find our place.
With every connection, the world disappears,
In the love we nurture, through all our years.

# The Theater of Together

In the spotlight's warm embrace,
We share our dreams with grace.
Each laugh a note in our song,
Together where we belong.

Curtains rise, hearts align,
Life's stage a spark divine.
With every glance, a story told,
In our souls, warmth against the cold.

The audience, a sea of eyes,
Captive to our sweet goodbyes.
In whispers soft, our hopes ignite,
Creating magic in the night.

Dancing shadows, hand in hand,
In this space, together we stand.
Every moment, a fleeting play,
Forever etched, never to fray.

As the final bow is near,
We hold close what we hold dear.
In this theater, love will sing,
United in every little thing.

## **Designs of Deep Affection**

In the fabric of our days,
We weave the sweetest praise.
Stitching dreams with gentle hands,
Creating love that understands.

Patterns bloom like flowers bright,
Delicate in morning light.
Each thread, a promise pure and true,
Bound together, me and you.

Colors blend in harmony,
Crafting our own symphony.
With every touch, our spirits rise,
Designs of love fill autumn skies.

In the quiet, we draw near,
Finding comfort in the clear.
Designs of laughter, tears, and trust,
A tapestry of love, a must.

Through the seasons, we will share,
Every heartbeat, every care.
In this art, forever stay,
A masterpiece that won't decay.

## The Sanctuary of Shared Stories

In the corners of the night,
Whispers drift like soft light.
Every tale, a sacred thread,
Binding what's been left unsaid.

Beneath stars, we gather close,
In this haven, we chose.
Each story whispers peace and pain,
A tapestry of joy and rain.

Listen deep, these tales unfold,
Of adventures brave and bold.
From the past, we draw our strength,
In shared words, we find our length.

Turn the pages, find the truth,
In every tale, a glimpse of youth.
The sanctuary holds our fears,
Echoes soft of laughter and tears.

As the dawn begins to rise,
In each heart, our stories lie.
Together, we face what's ahead,
In this sanctuary, we're led.

## **Explorations in Emotional Landscapes**

In the valleys of our minds,
We explore what love defines.
Mountains high, rivers wide,
Every feeling, a joyful ride.

Beneath the sky so vast and blue,
We carve paths for me and you.
With each step, a new uncover,
In emotional lands, we discover.

Fields of laughter, forests of tears,
Holding close all our fears.
With every peak, we find the light,
Guiding each other through the night.

In the echoes of our hearts,
We create a map, love imparts.
Through every twist, through every turn,
In this land, forever we yearn.

As we venture, hand in hand,
Navigating this rich, wild land.
Emotional landscapes, alive and free,
Together, we'll always be.

## **Blueprints of Belonging**

In the heart of every home,
Walls whisper secrets, softly known.
Footsteps echo through the halls,
Each moment treasured, love enthralls.

Connections woven, thread by thread,
Memories linger, softly spread.
A tapestry of shared delight,
Guiding us through the darkest night.

Laughter dances on the breeze,
Roots entwined like ancient trees.
Here we stand, no need to roam,
In this embrace, we find our home.

Through storms and sunshine, hand in hand,
Together we make our brave stand.
In the warmth of belonging's glow,
Our spirits soar, we surely grow.

Every heartbeat sings a song,
Of finding where our souls belong.
In the blueprints of our lives,
The love we build forever thrives.

# The Gallery of Gifts Given

In the corners of our hearts,
Lie treasures hidden, just like arts.
Each gesture, small, a bright array,
A gallery of gifts displayed.

Painted with kindness, strokes of grace,
A smile in every time and place.
With every word, a brush does glide,
Colors blend, and worlds collide.

Stories told, a canvas bright,
Gifts we've shared, with pure delight.
From hands to hearts, we freely give,
A legacy of love we live.

These moments shine, like stars above,
In this gallery, we find our love.
The beauty of what life imparts,
A masterpiece of gentle hearts.

As life unfolds, each gift we choose,
In this exhibit, we can't lose.
With open arms, our spirits lift,
Inviting all into this gift.

## Inventing Connection

Across the distance, I reach for you,
In silence, words are born anew.
In every glance, a spark ignites,
Inventing bonds, our hearts take flight.

The spaces between, so rich and wide,
With laughter as our steady guide.
Together, crafting dreams and schemes,
A tapestry woven with shared dreams.

In whispered hopes and gentle sighs,
We find the truth behind our eyes.
Like rivers flowing into the sea,
These connections form our destiny.

A dance of souls, entwined and free,
A testament to you and me.
With every step, our spirits blend,
In this journey, there's no end.

As we explore this vast expanse,
Every moment, a cherished chance.
Creating bonds that feel like home,
In harmony, together we roam.

## The Forge of Feelings

In the furnace of the heart, we try,
To mold the truth beneath the sky.
With passion's fire, we shape and bend,
The forge of feelings knows no end.

Each spark ignites a vibrant flame,
In every joy, we stake our claim.
Through trials faced, we learn to yield,
In the heat, our souls are healed.

With every blow, a lesson learned,
The heat of life, a passion burned.
From molten clay, we form our dreams,
Crafting life from love's pure streams.

Together we stand, side by side,
As we navigate this wondrous ride.
Through laughter, tears, and all in between,
The forge of feelings keeps us keen.

In this workshop of our hearts,
We build connections, play our parts.
Forging bonds that ever grow,
In the warmth of love, we find our flow.

## Lessons in the Art of Embrace

In the quiet folds of night,
We find warmth in soft whispers,
Like a canvas in gentle light,
Embraces paint love's character.

Hands entwined, a sacred bond,
Every pulse a heartbeat shared,
In the silence, our hearts respond,
Every moment, truly bared.

To hold close is to learn deep,
The secrets in tender gestures,
Through warmth, through shared dreams we leap,
Embracing life's sweet adventures.

Lessons taught, not in the words,
But in the closeness that we share,
In the language of undisturbed birds,
A rhythm that's beyond compare.

So take my hand, let's drift away,
In the art of embrace we'll thrive,
Through the night, until the day,
In our hearts, we feel alive.

## The Chemistry of Kindred Spirits

In the alchemy of our laughter,
Two souls blend like moonlit streams,
Creating dreams of ever after,
Kindred spirits weave their themes.

Fires glow in shared delight,
Each glance ignites a love untold,
In the dark, we find our light,
Our hearts, a treasure to behold.

Atoms dance in cosmic play,
With every word, connection grows,
Science of love leads the way,
Through trials, true affection flows.

In the lab of life, we experiment,
Mixing joy with laughter's balm,
Through every moment we present,
Each heartbeat feels so calm.

So here's to bonds that surely last,
In the chemistry of our souls,
With every shared future cast,
Together, we feel whole.

## Studies in the Language of Hearts

Written in whispers and sighs,
The language of love softly speaks,
In the depths of our longing eyes,
A bond that grows with every week.

Through gestures, our hearts reveal,
The verses that words cannot say,
In every touch, a truth we feel,
Guiding us along the way.

Eloquent in the quiet of night,
In absence, our hearts grow fonder,
Translating love's pure light,
A connection that draws us yonder.

Page by page, we turn our fate,
Writing stories of joy and tears,
In every chapter we create,
Through laughter, love, and fears.

So let us study this grand art,
In the language that flows from within,
With every beat, we're never apart,
Our journey, where love begins.

## Experimenting with Affection

In the lab of everyday life,
We mix kindness with a smile,
Finding joy, away from strife,
Creating magic all the while.

Testing limits of our hearts,
With affection as our guide,
Every gesture, a work of art,
Trusting love, we brave the tide.

In every hug, we find explore,
Infinite ways to connect,
Like curious minds wanting more,
Through every kiss, we reflect.

Discoveries in every moment,
Chemistry borne from pure delight,
With each touch, there's new content,
Experimenting in the night.

So let's create, in love's embrace,
A world where affection thrives,
In this wondrous, sacred space,
Together, our passion drives.

## A Garden of Intimacies

In a garden of whispers, we tend the blooms,
Each petal a secret, where love gently looms.
Sunlight dances softly on leaves made of lace,
In the heart's quiet corner, we find our own space.

With roots intertwined, our spirits take flight,
Nurtured by laughter, we grow in the light.
The fragrance of memories fills the warm air,
As we wander the pathways, in love without care.

The shadows grow longer as twilight arrives,
Painting dreams in the dusk where our hope thrives.
Hand in hand, we walk through the soft twilight,
In a garden of intimacies, all feels just right.

Every flower a promise, each vine a new chance,
In this sacred space, our souls slip and dance.
Together we flourish, though storms may arise,
In this garden of intimacies, love never dies.

# The Map of Togetherness

In the folds of paper, every crease holds a dream,
Paths drawn with fervor, where hearts often beam.
With ink of affection, we chart out our way,
Through valleys of laughter, to where night meets day.

The compass of trust always points to your side,
In the journey of life, with you as my guide.
Through mountains of trials, we navigate bold,
With warmth in our hearts, in the chill and the cold.

Each moment a milestone, each glance a new start,
In the map of togetherness, you're always my heart.
We travel the distance; we shelter the pain,
In the beauty of moments, our love will remain.

Crossing rivers of doubt, we find shores of gold,
In laughter and joy, our story unfolds.
With every step taken, our bond grows more tight,
In the map of togetherness, we're guided by light.

## Uncharted Territories of the Heart

In the wild of emotion, we wander so free,
Through uncharted territories, just you and me.
With courage as our lantern, we light up the dark,
Finding peace in the chaos, igniting a spark.

Every heartbeat a whisper, every glance a new realm,
Navigating the currents, together we helm.
With each touch a treasure, each kiss a new start,
Exploring the depth of these uncharted parts.

In silence, we listen to what lies beneath,
Unearthing the beauty of life in our wreath.
With hands intertwined, we face what may come,
In the uncharted territories, our spirits are one.

As stars adorn the night, our journey unfolds,
With stories unspoken, and dreams yet untold.
In the richness of love, we find out who we are,
Bound by our passions, we'll follow the stars.

# **Insights from the Affectionate Mind**

From the depths of affection, thoughts take their flight,
Wings of understanding, in the softest of light.
Each moment a canvas, painted with care,
Crafting insights that linger in the warm air.

In the nuances of silence, meanings arise,
Through unspoken bonds, we uncover the ties.
With empathy guiding, we dive deep within,
In the realm of our hearts, where connections begin.

The tenderest feelings, like whispers in spring,
Echoes of comfort that love always brings.
In this affectionate mind, we find clarity,
A landscape of feelings, where souls dance so free.

With every shared secret, the walls start to fade,
In insights of affection, our foundation is laid.
Building a bridge wherever we roam,
In the heart of connection, we always find home.

## Captures of Caring

In gentle hands, the warmest touch,
A whispered word means oh so much.
In every glance, a story shared,
A tender heart that always cared.

Through trials faced and shadows cast,
A bond is formed that's built to last.
In laughter's song and sorrow's tide,
Together, always side by side.

With simple acts, love's essence glows,
A kind embrace that softly shows.
In every moment, big and small,
True caring nurtures, binds us all.

When skies are gray and spirits low,
The light of love begins to grow.
With open arms and hearts so true,
We find our strength in me and you.

So let us capture every thrill,
The magic moments that we fill.
For in our hearts, we all shall keep,
The memories of love so deep.

## **Architects of Affection**

With blueprint hearts, we sketch our dreams,
Building bridges, or so it seems.
Compassion's tools, our hands employ,
To forge the ties of love and joy.

Each loving act, a stone we lay,
Creating paths where shadows play.
In every word, a fortress strong,
We craft a place where we belong.

Together, side by side, we strive,
To keep our cherished hopes alive.
With every plan, a vision clear,
We mold our future, year by year.

In laughter's echo, blueprints made,
Through trials faced, our dreams won't fade.
As architects with hearts so bright,
We shape our world with love and light.

So let us build with care and grace,
A legacy that time won't erase.
For in our hearts, affection thrives,
The masterpiece of our lives.

## The Odyssey of Opened Hearts

In journeys vast, our souls take flight,
With open hearts, we seek the light.
Through storm and calm, we find our way,
An odyssey of love each day.

With every step, new paths we trace,
Embracing joy, leaving no space.
In laughter's wake and tears we share,
We navigate with utmost care.

Adventure calls in whispers sweet,
As we discover love's heartbeat.
With open hearts, we welcome all,
In unity, we stand up tall.

Through trials faced and mountains climbed,
Each moment shared, we're interlined.
In every tale, our spirits soar,
An odyssey forevermore.

So take my hand, let's venture wide,
In opened hearts, there's naught to hide.
For love's great journey knows no end,
Together, dear, let's always mend.

## The Weaving of Warmth

In threads of gold, our stories spun,
With every smile, two hearts become one.
A tapestry of joyful deeds,
We weave together, meeting needs.

Each gentle touch, a fiber bright,
In shared experiences, we find light.
With every laugh, a stitch so fine,
Creating warmth through tales divine.

In storms that come, we stand secure,
Our woven hearts forever pure.
With kindness' thread, we mend the fray,
Together, come what may.

As seasons change and life unfolds,
Our fabric rich with stories told.
Through love, we weave, both strong and true,
A quilt of warmth, just me and you.

So let us craft with hands so skilled,
A legacy of love fulfilled.
For in this weaving, bonds we find,
A lasting warmth, a love entwined.

## The Canvas of Loving Moments

In twilight's glow, we find our grace,
Each whisper shared, a sweet embrace.
The brush of hearts, a soft caress,
Painting time in love's finesse.

Laughter dances on the air,
Creating memories, rich and rare.
In every glance, a story spun,
Together, we shine like the sun.

With every heartbeat, colors blend,
A masterpiece that has no end.
In gentle strokes, our souls align,
A canvas bright, by love's design.

As seasons change, our palette shifts,
Yet in each hue, true joy uplifts.
We gather moments, heart by heart,
In this grand work, we play our part.

Forever framed in love's embrace,
Each loving moment, finds its place.
In this gallery, side by side,
Through every storm, we shall abide.

## Notes from the Field of Feelings

In the meadow, emotions sway,
Thoughts like petals drift away.
Echoes of laughter, whispers of cheer,
Capture the essence of those held dear.

Amidst the wildflowers, we discover,
The ties that bind sister and brother.
Every tear, a droplet of light,
In this field, darkness takes flight.

From joy to sorrow, we navigate,
Through tangled paths, we celebrate.
In the silence, a song remains,
A symphony born from our pains.

By the riverside, dreams take flight,
Chasing stars in the depth of night.
With every pulse, our hearts still sing,
In this field, love's journey takes wing.

In the quiet, truths unfold,
These notes of feeling, soft yet bold.
In harmony, we learn to grow,
With each heartbeat, we let it show.

## The Book of Trials and Triumphs

Each page turned, a tale unfolds,
Of battles fought and dreams retold.
In shadows deep, a light shines through,
With every scar, we start anew.

Through storms endured and rivers crossed,
We gather strength despite the cost.
In the silence, resilience grows,
With every step, our spirit flows.

The chapters hold both tears and smiles,
In every struggle, we walk miles.
Through peaks and valleys, we find our way,
With ink of courage, we write each day.

For in the trials, wisdom gleams,
In every setback, we dare to dream.
A testament to the heart's great fight,
This book is filled with boundless light.

We pen our story, line by line,
Through every trial, our souls align.
In triumph's glow, we find our voice,
With love and hope, we make our choice.

## Discoveries in Devotional Spaces

In quiet corners, peace resides,
Where whispered prayers and hope abides.
With open hearts, we seek the divine,
In sacred moments, our spirits align.

Through gentle breaths, we find our way,
In stillness, worries drift away.
Each thought a ripple, soft and clear,
In these spaces, love draws near.

With fragrant blooms and candlelight,
We journey inward, bask in the light.
In every sigh, a promise flows,
In these discoveries, our faith grows.

The heart's devotion knows no end,
In these spaces, we transcend.
Each joy and sorrow gently shared,
Through every moment, we are paired.

With eyes wide open, we embrace the grace,
In every heartbeat, we find our place.
In sacred beauty, we come alive,
In these spaces, our spirits thrive.

## The Theater of Tenderness

In whispers soft, we tread the stage,
A dance of hearts, a fleeting page.
With every glance, a story blooms,
In this sweet space, love brightly looms.

The curtains rise, our secrets shared,
Hand in hand, no burdens bared.
Each act unfolds a tender light,
In the embrace of starry night.

With every tear, a joy concealed,
Our laughter echoes, fate revealed.
Together we create our play,
In this theater, we always stay.

As shadows drift, and dreams arise,
We find our truth in loving sighs.
In silent breaths, our spirits blend,
In tenderness, we find the end.

This stage will hold our tales unsaid,
In gentle hearts, our love is spread.
Forever bound, we take our bow,
In this theater, the time is now.

## **Kaleidoscope of Intimate Moments**

In fleeting glances, colors swirl,
With each touch, the night's a pearl.
A tapestry of laughter spun,
In soft embrace, two souls are one.

The world refracts in vibrant hues,
Where whispers dance, and dreams infuse.
A flicker here, a twinkle there,
In every glance, a world laid bare.

Heartbeats synchronize in sync,
In shared silence, we deeply think.
Our eyes collide, a spark ignites,
In this kaleidoscope, love delights.

Moments shift, yet still we stare,
In this vivid realm, we lay bare.
Each flash a memory we will keep,
In the depths where feelings seep.

Through every lens, we paint the night,
In shades of joy, and pure delight.
Together bound in vibrant art,
Our love's the canvas of the heart.

## The Map of Merging Lives

Two paths converge beneath the stars,
A journey shared, no distance far.
With every step, our footprints blend,
In this map, no need to mend.

As rivers flow into the sea,
We find in love, our destiny.
The roads we've traveled intertwine,
In every twist, your heart is mine.

In laughter's echoes, and soft sighs,
We lay the course beneath the skies.
With every turn, new wonders thrive,
In this exploration, we come alive.

Together onward, hand in hand,
Through valleys deep and shifting sand.
No paths too rough, no skies too gray,
In this map, we find our way.

For each new dawn, a fresh insight,
Guided by love's eternal light.
With every journey we embark,
In merging lives, we leave our mark.

## The Frame of Found Hearts

In tender frames, our story's drawn,
With every smile, a brand new dawn.
Captured moments, love defined,
In this picture, two souls aligned.

The warmth of you, a gentle trace,
In time's embrace, we find our place.
Each glance a brush, each kiss a hue,
A masterpiece where dreams come true.

Beneath the stars, we paint the night,
In strokes of joy, our hearts take flight.
A canvas rich with shaded fears,
In this artwork, love's joy appears.

With frames adorned by life's sweet song,
Together, where our hearts belong.
In every sigh, and every glance,
This frame of love, our sacred dance.

As seasons change, our art remains,
In vibrant colors, joy sustains.
In this frame, forever we stand,
In the gallery of life's grand plan.

# The Alchemy of Intimacy

In whispers soft, our secrets blend,
Two souls entwined, an endless trend.
Hearts in rhythm, a silent dance,
In every glance, a fleeting chance.

With every touch, a spark ignites,
Transforming shadows into lights.
In sacred spaces, trust grows deep,
In shared silence, we gently seep.

Through laughter's grace, and sorrow's tears,
We forge a bond that defies years.
In laughter's echo, love's sweet song,
Together we find where we belong.

In moments fleeting, we intertwine,
Two hearts as one, a true divine.
Each breath a promise, each sigh a vow,
In love's embrace, we're lost somehow.

## Navigating Vulnerability's Terrain

To bare our souls, a daunting quest,
Yet in that truth, we find our best.
With tender hearts, we tread the line,
Where fear and hope in silence twine.

In broken whispers, we discover strength,
Together, we'll go to any length.
With open arms, we face the storm,
In fragile trust, our spirits warm.

Each shared moment, a fragile thread,
In vulnerability, no tears unshed.
Through every bruise, we heal anew,
In honesty, our love shines through.

So let us walk this winding path,
Hand in hand, igniting the aftermath.
In every stumble, while we may fall,
We rise together, loving all.

## The Science of Shared Dreams

In twilight hues, we craft our plans,
Two hearts aligned, with joined hands.
In starlit skies, ambitions soar,
Together we seek to dream and explore.

With every thought, our visions merge,
In unison, our hopes emerge.
Through trials faced and joys imparted,
In shared dreams, our journeys started.

In whispers soft, we dare to dream,
With faith in us, we find the beam.
Navigating paths of life's great flow,
In every challenge, our courage grows.

So let's sketch futures on cosmic sand,
With laughter, tears—together we stand.
With every heartbeat, we'll make it real,
In shared dreams, our fates congeal.

## **Instruction Manual for Tender Moments**

First, be present, shed the crowd,
In whispered tones, love's voice is loud.
Embrace the silence, hold it near,
In gentle gestures, we persevere.

Take time to listen, hear each sigh,
In this stillness, our spirits fly.
With simple words, weave your art,
A touch of kindness can warm the heart.

In laughter shared, find the grace,
In every glance, a soft embrace.
Let honesty bloom, tender and true,
In every moment, create anew.

So turn the page, and start again,
With open hearts, love's sweet refrain.
In tender moments, life is bright,
Together we shine, a dazzling light.

## Discoveries in the Dance

In dim-lit rooms we find our way,
With gentle steps, we sway and play.
The music wraps us, soft and grand,
In every beat, we understand.

Your laugh, a sparkle in the night,
Draws me closer, feels so right.
With every twirl, our souls ignite,
A shared rhythm, pure delight.

Through whispered moves our spirits flow,
Each fleeting glance, a warm glow.
I lead you here, then you pull me near,
In this dance, we lose all fear.

Among the shadows, vibrant dreams,
In perfect time, a dance of themes.
With every spin, our hearts collide,
In this moment, love won't hide.

The world outside fades to a blur,
In our embrace, everything stirs.
Each step a promise, each turn a chance,
Forever lost in this sweet dance.

## The Symphony of Shared Moments

In laughter's echo, we find our song,
Each note a memory, where we belong.
Time slows down as we share a glance,
In unison, our hearts do dance.

The warmth of your hand, a gentle touch,
Speaks volumes louder than words can clutch.
We weave a tapestry, rich and bright,
In the quiet corners of the night.

With every sigh, stories unfold,
Like pages of life, precious and bold.
In fleeting moments, forever cherished,
In this symphony, our fears have perished.

Together we build a resonant space,
Where time stands still, a sacred place.
Harmonies blend, our spirits unite,
In this symphony, everything feels right.

So let us gather the whispers we find,
In shared moments, our souls aligned.
A melody sweet, like twilight's embrace,
In the dance of our lives, we find grace.

## Portraits of a Connection

In a canvas of moments, we paint our dreams,
With brushstrokes of laughter, soft silken seams.
Each color a heartbeat, each shade a sigh,
In the gallery of us, where memories lie.

Captured in frames, the smiles we wear,
Moments suspended, a love laid bare.
With whispers of joy, the hues intertwine,
In this portrait, your heart feels like mine.

Through the lenses of time, we focus our sights,
On the beauty found in the quiet nights.
Each glance a treasure, each touch divine,
In the art of connection, the stars align.

So paint me your dreams, with strokes sincere,
Through shadows and light, I hold you near.
In every detail, our story's told,
A masterpiece born from hearts of gold.

In the gallery of moments, let's forever roam,
Creating portraits, an everlasting home.
And as time unfolds, our colors will blend,
In this beautiful journey, love knows no end.

## Chemistry Between Us

In the glance we share, a spark ignites,
With every word, the tension excites.
Two energies collide, magnetic and true,
In this dance of fate, it's me and you.

A rhythm unknown, yet deeply felt,
In the warmth of your gaze, my heart does melt.
Like particles drawn in an unseen force,
In the chemistry shared, we find our course.

With laughter's charge, we light the night,
In the glow of our bond, everything feels right.
Through electric moments, our passions soar,
In this beautiful madness, we crave for more.

Every whisper a spark, igniting the air,
In the silence that follows, you're always there.
Two elements bound, an unbreakable link,
In this chemistry, we forever think.

 let us explore this wondrous connection,
ith each heartbeat, a sweet resurrection.
 dance of our souls, a world to create,
 chemistry between us, we celebrate.

## The Art of Heartfelt Growth

In the garden where dreams take flight,
Seeds of hope bloom in the gentle light.
Roots entwined beneath the earth's embrace,
Each moment nurtures a sacred space.

Petals unfurl with a tender grace,
Colors emerge in a soft, warm trace.
Time weaves stories of joy and strife,
In the tapestry of a blossomed life.

Through storms that test our will to stand,
We find the strength held in gentle hands.
As seasons change, so do we learn,
From every heartbreak, our hearts return.

Embrace the journey, share the tears,
For in each setback, wisdom nears.
With every challenge, we cultivate,
The art of growth in love's own fate.

So cherish the moments, both small and grand,
With every heartbeat, together we stand.
Through the trials, our spirits will soar,
In the vibrant dance of forevermore.

## Experiments in Emotion

In a lab of feelings, we mix and blend,
Hopes like chemicals, curves that extend.
Joy bubbles up like a fizzy delight,
While sorrow settles in shadows of night.

We measure laughter in heartbeats fast,
Counting the echoes of memories past.
Each reaction provokes a new way,
To understand how we feel and play.

With courage, we calculate love's sweet cost,
In the data of moments we thought we lost.
Every hypothesis tested with care,
Bringing us closer, a bond we share.

Through trials and errors, we learn to cope,
Mixing despair with a recipe of hope.
In the beaker of life, emotions ignite,
Creating a spectrum of wrong and right.

So let's conduct our own heartfelt tests,
Embrace the chaos, let passion rest.
For every experiment leads us to see,
The depth of our hearts, wild and free.

## Whispers of Tenderness

In the quiet corners of the night,
Softly spoken words take delicate flight.
Like a gentle breeze through the trees,
Whispers of tenderness wrap and tease.

In the hush of dusk, where secrets lie,
Promises linger like stars in the sky.
Each touch, a promise, a silent vow,
Caught in the moment, here and now.

With every glance, stories unfold,
Tender truths waiting to be told.
A language of warmth that's felt, not heard,
In the space between, emotions stirred.

Embrace the calm, let the silence speak,
In the stillness, it's connection we seek.
A heartbeat echoes in the tender night,
Whispers of love, a sweet delight.

So breathe in deep these moments rare,
In quiet surrender, we lay our care.
For in the tenderness, we shall find,
The whispers of love, eternally entwined.

## Bonds Forged in Fire

Through the flames of trials, we stand as one,
In the heat of conflict, a battle begun.
Forged in the fires of rhetoric fierce,
With every challenge, our souls we pierce.

Molten hearts blend in the furnace bright,
Strengthening ties in the lustrous light.
The embers of courage, they flicker and glow,
A testament to love's unwavering flow.

With every spark, we've learned to defend,
Life's fiery moments, they shape and mend.
Through ashes and smoke, our spirits rise,
Bonds made resilient, with love as our prize.

United in purpose, through thick and thin,
Together we conquer, together we win.
For in the inferno, we find our grace,
Crafted in warmth, our forever place.

So let the flames dance, let the fires burn,
In their fierce light, deeper lessons we learn.
For bonds forged in fire are strong and true,
A beacon of hope, ever bright, ever new.

## **Journey Through Affection's Labyrinth**

In shadows deep, we start to roam,
Through mazes forged in whispers, home.
Each turn reveals a gentle sigh,
Where love's sweet echo won't deny.

With every corner, hearts entwine,
A tapestry of souls that shine.
Hand in hand, we weave our way,
To light that guides our warm ballet.

The walls are lined with dreams we share,
Each secret held with tender care.
In every step, affection grows,
As petals bloom, the garden knows.

Through tangled paths, we face our fears,
A dance of joy, a clash of tears.
Yet in this maze, we find our truth,
The map of love drawn from our youth.

So let us wander, side by side,
In this labyrinth where hearts reside.
The journey's long, yet worth the run,
For love, we find, has just begun.

## In the Workshop of Hearts


In a space where dreams collide,
We craft our hopes, no need to hide.
Each heartbeat turns into a tool,
In this workshop, love's the rule.

With hands that shape and minds that mold,
We build connections, brave and bold.
Each whispered thought, a spark ignites,
In the glow of shared delights.

The bench is strewn with shared regrets,
Yet here we learn, the heart forgets.
A place where trust can softly grow,
With every strike, we feel the flow.

With every project, strong and frail,
We learn to brace against the gale.
Together, then, we find our art,
Creating pieces of the heart.

This workshop thrives on all we share,
In every laugh, a breath of air.
Our hands may tire, but never part,
For love's the language of the heart.

## The Classroom of Connection

In this classroom of the soul,
We gather thoughts to make us whole.
Each lesson learned, a bridge we build,
With trust and care, our hearts fulfilled.

The chalkboard's filled with dreams in ink,
Where every moment helps us think.
With every word, a bond we tie,
In this space where spirits fly.

The tests of time may come and go,
Yet here we plant the seeds to grow.
In friendship's realm, we find our strength,
As bonds expand, we share our length.

From every corner, wisdom shines,
In laughter shared, our love defines.
We learn to ask, to touch, to feel,
As hearts connect, our truths reveal.

So sit beside me, learn this art,
Together we can play our part.
In this classroom, let's embrace,
The joy of love, a warm embrace.

## Secrets of the Soul's Curriculum

We gather here to share our tales,
In whispered tones, the heart unveils.
Each secret penned with care and grace,
A journey through this sacred space.

The syllabus of trust unfolds,
With lessons rich, both new and old.
In every glance, a story told,
In every touch, a warmth to hold.

With every question, answers bloom,
In open hearts, we find the room.
For every scar, a tale to weave,
In the fabric of what we believe.

The tests of love may come and go,
Yet through it all, our spirits grow.
In the depths of pain and joy we live,
The soul's curriculum teaches to give.

So let us share these secrets bright,
In the embrace of starry night.
Together we'll uncover the thread,
Of love's great lesson, gently led.

## The Network of Nuance

In whispers soft, we weave our ties,
Through threads of thought, where silence lies.
A gentle touch, a knowing glance,
In hidden depths, we find our dance.

Beneath the surface, currents flow,
In shadowed realms, our feelings grow.
Each heartbeat echoes, loud yet small,
A whispered truth connects us all.

With every word, a layer peels,
Revealing what our heart conceals.
In subtle signs, we come alive,
For in this web, we learn to thrive.

A map of dreams, a quest for light,
In shades of dusk, we spark the night.
Each nuance formed, a story told,
In vibrant hues, our lives unfold.

Together strong, we shape the stream,
In tethered grace, we find our dream.
In this vast net, we gently sway,
In shared embrace, we find our way.

## Doodles of Delightful Touches

In margins bright, our laughter dwells,
With playful lines, our story swells.
Each little mark, a joy unbound,
In every sketch, sweet memories found.

A swirl of color, a burst of cheer,
In every stroke, our dreams appear.
With whimsy's grace, we dance and play,
In doodled moments, we find our way.

Lines intertwine, like fingers clasped,
In scribbled joy, the heart is clasped.
With each embrace, a spark ignites,
In laughter's glow, our spirit lights.

A canvas bright, imagination's spree,
In quirky shapes, we both agree.
With every touch, love's essence flows,
In every corner, our joy just grows.

So let us doodle through the day,
In every smile, in every sway.
With vibrant hearts, we'll never rush,
In life's sweet art, our hearts will hush.

## The Space Between Hearts

In silence held, a world exists,
Between our souls, a gentle mist.
In breaths we share, the stillness reigns,
A sacred space where love remains.

In gaps unspoken, trust takes flight,
In shadows cast, we find our light.
Each tender pause, an invitation,
A whispered bond, a slow creation.

Between the notes, our song unfolds,
In every beat, a story told.
In quiet moments, warmth is found,
With open hearts, we are spellbound.

An empty space, yet filled with grace,
Where words may fail, love finds its place.
In longing sighs and fleeting glances,
We find our truth in silent dances.

Each heartbeat shared, a cosmos wide,
In this sweet void, we do abide.
For in the space where feelings start,
Lies the deep pulse of every heart.

# **Reconstructing the Framework of Bonds**

With gentle hands, we forge anew,
In broken threads, a vibrant hue.
Rebuilding trust, with pieces small,
In every stitch, we rise from fall.

Each crack a tale, each flaw a guide,
In woven paths, our hearts confide.
Through trials faced, we grow our roots,
In every knot, love's essence suits.

From ashes rise, we breathe again,
In whispered hopes, we grow the grain.
With steady hearts, we find our core,
In love's embrace, we seek for more.

The framework strong, yet ever light,
In shifting sands, we grasp the bright.
With every trial, our spirits soar,
In tangled bonds, we learn to explore.

So hand in hand, we craft our way,
Through storms and sun, together stay.
Reconstructing dreams, we build our house,
In love's firm grip, we make our vows.

## The Symphony of Synchronized Souls

In the quiet night, we find our tune,
Hearts entwined under the silver moon.
Each note we play, a vibrant light,
Together we soar, taking flight.

With whispers soft, we share our dreams,
A melody built on hopeful themes.
Hands held tight, we dance so free,
In harmony, just you and me.

Through tides of change, our song persists,
In life's grand show, we coexist.
With every chord, our spirits blend,
A symphony that will never end.

The world may falter, shadows may fall,
But we remain, standing tall.
In every beat, our love resounds,
Eternal echoes, joy abounds.

So let the music forever play,
In synchronized souls, we'll find our way.
With hearts aligned, we rise anew,
Together, always, me and you.

# The Garden of Growth

In the soil of dreams, we plant our seeds,
Nurtured by hope, and gentle deeds.
With patient hands, we tend the sprouts,
A garden where love continuously shouts.

Sunlight cascades, warm and bright,
Encouraging roots to stretch in flight.
Rain falls softly, like tender care,
Washing the worries, leaving us bare.

Each petal unfolds, a story in bloom,
From tiny beginnings to a vibrant room.
Colors will flourish, a sight to behold,
In the garden of growth, our dreams unfold.

Time moves gently, seasons will change,
But our bond remains, forever in range.
Through winds of struggle, we stand so strong,
In unity, where we all belong.

So let us tend to this sacred place,
With love and laughter, our hearts embrace.
In the garden of growth, we rise as one,
Together forever, our journey begun.

## **Formulas for Flourishing**

In the canvas of life, we brush with intent,
Crafting equations where love is lent.
With each little step, we pave the way,
Formulas of joy, come what may.

Patience and trust, ingredients rare,
Mix them with kindness, a recipe fair.
Stir in some laughter, let worries out,
Flourishing hearts, that's what it's about.

Each moment adds value, a piece of the whole,
Together we blossom, nurturing the soul.
In the lab of living, time's our best friend,
Forms of connection, that never can end.

Count the blessings, let gratitude flow,
Finding the beauty in all that we grow.
Here lies the magic, in each heartfelt glance,
In formulas shared, we find our dance.

So let's craft a life, with love as the core,
Discovering treasures on every shore.
In the formulas for flourishing, we ignite,
Together we'll shine, brilliant and bright.

## The Chronicle of Connection

Turn the pages, let stories unfold,
Each chapter a journey, with treasures untold.
In the book of life, our tales intertwine,
The chronicle of connection, so divine.

Through laughter and tears, we write our lines,
Moments shared like the best of wines.
In every heartbeat, a rhythm we find,
A beautiful bond that's forever aligned.

With ink of memories, we sketch our paths,
Through trials and triumphs, the aftermaths.
A tapestry woven, with threads of gold,
In the chronicles of old, our stories told.

As pages turn, let us never forget,
The ties that bind, our hearts in duet.
In the quiet whispers, there's strength to be found,
A connection that echoes, profound.

So let the narrative flow, bright and bold,
In the chronicle of connection, we'll behold.
Together we write, both you and I,
A story of love that will never die.

## **Heartstrings Unraveled**

In the quiet, whispers cling,
Threads of love now start to sing.
Fragile bonds, a dance of chance,
In every smile, in every glance.

Tears like rain on window panes,
Softly touch the deepest pains.
Every heartbeat tells a tale,
Of love's echo, frail and pale.

Promises woven through the night,
Fading softly, lost in light.
Yet in the shadows, hope remains,
Loving memories break the chains.

With every thread that starts to fray,
A reminder of yesterday.
For heartstrings pulled can still renew,
As love unfolds, forever true.

So gather close, the stories shared,
In every ache, the love we dared.
Though unraveled, it finds its way,
In a tapestry of yesterday.

## The Chemistry of Connection

Two souls collide in starry night,
A dance ignites, pure and bright.
Footsteps echo, hearts align,
In this moment, you are mine.

Your laughter sparks a thousand flames,
In silent glances, love's true names.
A heartbeat felt within the skin,
Every pulse, where dreams begin.

Chemistry flows like rivers wide,
In every tear, in every tide.
You are the sun, my guiding star,
In your embrace, I've come so far.

Moments linger, time stands still,
In your eyes, a magic thrill.
Lay down the fears that night's begun,
For in this space, we are as one.

Cocooned in warmth, beneath the moon,
Every heartbeat, a tender tune.
The chemistry that binds us tight,
Is love's sweet song in the night.

## **Lessons in the Embrace**

In the embrace, we find our peace,
Softened edges gently cease.
Every heartbeat, wisdom shared,
In tender arms, love's truth declared.

Through laughter and through gentle sighs,
We unearth dreams beneath the skies.
Lessons whispered, shadows flee,
In your hold, I am set free.

Moments etched like ink on skin,
All the battles lost and win.
Every touch, a silent vow,
In this embrace, we live right now.

Life's a journey, winding, long,
In your arms, I feel so strong.
Every lesson learned with grace,
A testament in our embrace.

So hold me close, let time stand still,
In every breath, my heart you fill.
The lessons blossom, fully grown,
In this embrace, we've found a home.

## **Echoes of Affection**

In every smile, a memory glows,
Whispers of love, where the heart goes.
Echoes linger in the air,
Soft reminders of love laid bare.

Through the shadows, your voice I hear,
A melody sweet, drawing near.
Time may fade, but feelings stay,
In every heartbeat, come what may.

Afternoon sun, warm on my skin,
In every moment, I feel you within.
Echoes dance in the twilight's gleam,
A symphony of a shared dream.

With every sunrise, tales unfold,
In every glance, a love retold.
Though distances may stretch and bend,
In the echoes, we never end.

So let the world spin fast or slow,
In my heart, you'll always know.
Echoes of affection remain,
A timeless bond, a sweet refrain.

## **The Blueprint of Bonds**

In the quiet of the night,
Plans of love unfold bright.
Lines drawn with hope and care,
A map of hearts laid bare.

Every smile a gentle trace,
Every glance a warm embrace.
Crafting ties that intertwine,
Two souls to forever align.

Through storms and sunny days,
We dance in countless ways.
With laughter as our glue,
In every hue, love's true.

Building dreams, brick by brick,
Every moment, every tick.
In this workshop of the heart,
Together we'll never part.

With every laugh and every sigh,
We sketch the reasons why.
Crafting love, layer by layer,
In this design, we'll always share.

## Experiments in Endearment

In the lab of sweet endeavor,
We mix the joys that tether.
With every glance we share,
We create an artful pair.

Test tubes filled with laughter,
Moments we chase after.
Each twinkle, every kiss,
A potion brewed in bliss.

Chemicals of trust in play,
Countless mixtures every day.
With kindness, we ignite,
Creating sparks of delight.

Observing the heart's reaction,
In this charming attraction.
We gather data from our hearts,
In this dance, love never departs.

Each experiment a new embrace,
In this magical space.
With every trial, we refine,
Our love, a brilliant design.

## The Archive of Affectionate Acts

In this library of the heart,
Every moment plays its part.
Turning pages filled with grace,
Memories time cannot erase.

Each letter penned with care,
Whispers of love laid bare.
Every chapter tells a tale,
In this tribute, we will sail.

The bonds we forged with simple deeds,
Watering the love that feeds.
With notes and tokens stacked high,
In this archive, we will fly.

A collection of our dreams,
Rendered in soft moonbeams.
Ink that flows with every glance,
In this library, we dance.

As time unwinds its thread,
We read the love we've spread.
Forever bound, our will,
In this archive, hearts will fill.

## **Heartstrings in the Workshop**

In the workshop where hearts play,
We craft our love each day.
Strings of hope and dreams entwined,
Bound together, we align.

With gentle hands, we mold,
Stories of love yet untold.
Every heartbeat, every sigh,
An anthem to amplify.

Crafting joy with every tool,
Embracing love, so warm, so cool.
With laughter as our blueprint,
In this space, our love's imprint.

Nailing down our common ground,
In this rhythm, love is found.
Together, we shape the fate,
In this workshop, love creates.

As the day fades into night,
We find our dreams in flight.
With every piece aligned,
In this workshop, hearts combined.

## The Palette of Passion

Colors swirl beneath my skin,
Crimson dreams where love begins.
Each brush stroke, a heartbeat's song,
In this canvas, we belong.

Whispers paint the skies above,
Shades of warmth, a tale of love.
Vivid hues, they dance and blend,
In our art, a world to mend.

Splashes of joy, deep tints of pain,
Mixed emotions like summer rain.
Every color speaks our truth,
Together, we reclaim our youth.

On this palette, hearts ignite,
Passion glows in the dead of night.
Bound by strokes, by hues, by fate,
Our masterpiece we cultivate.

Through the chaos, beauty thrives,
In every shade, our spirit dives.
Here we stand, bold and free,
The palette whispers, you and me.

**Navigating the Seas of Devotion**

Waves crash softly on our dreams,
Guiding us through love's bright seams.
Sails unfurl as hearts align,
Together, we chase the divine.

Stars above, our compass clear,
In the night, I hold you near.
Tides may pull, yet we remain,
Through stormy seas, through joy and pain.

Anchored deep in trust and grace,
Navigating a sacred space.
With every turn, we learn and grow,
In this ocean's ebb and flow.

Currents strong, yet we are bold,
As passion's fire begins to unfold.
Hand in hand, we chart our course,
In love's embrace, we find our force.

As dawn breaks with golden hue,
Our hearts declare the love so true.
Navigating life's vast blue,
Forever sailing, me and you.

## The Architecture of Us

Bricks of laughter, walls of trust,
In every creak, in every gust.
Rooms filled with memories we create,
In this structure, we celebrate.

Windows wide to let light in,
Framing moments where we begin.
Each corner holds a whispered dream,
In our haven, love's sweet theme.

Roof of hopes that shelter nights,
Beneath its arch, we find our sights.
Foundations deep, built strong and true,
In this dwelling, it's me and you.

Hallways echo with our song,
Every step, where we belong.
Blueprint hearts, we lay it bare,
Together we rise, beyond compare.

In the silence, in the noise,
We create our home, full of joys.
The architecture of our souls,
Bound together, making us whole.

## **Curiosity in the Caress**

Fingers brush like softest feathers,
In the stillness, our hearts tether.
Eyes meet, a spark ignites,
Curiosity in endless nights.

Each caress, a question shared,
A dance of souls, beautifully paired.
Every touch, a story spun,
In this moment, we've just begun.

Whispers float on gentle breeze,
In the silence, we find our ease.
Exploring depths, skin to skin,
In this realm, our love begins.

Mapping curves with tender grace,
Charting paths, we find our place.
Every sigh, a tale of trust,
In our intimacy, we must.

Curiosity fuels the flame,
In each caress, we learn the name.
Of love so vast, so deeply true,
In every heartbeat, I find you.

## Epiphanies in Unity

In the silence of many, we find our voice,
Together we stand, in one shared choice.
Like threads intertwined, strong and tight,
In the tapestry of life, we bring the light.

Hearts beat in rhythm, a harmonious song,
In differences embraced, we all belong.
Awakening joy in the depths of our being,
Unity's beauty is truly worth seeing.

From shadows of doubt, we rise and reveal,
The power of trust becomes truly ideal.
In laughter and tears, in struggle and grace,
United we flourish, in love's warm embrace.

Each story a thread, a unique point of view,
We honor the past, and create something new.
For every epiphany shared in this space,
Is a moment of magic, a touch of pure grace.

# The Workshop of Whispers

In the quiet corners, where secrets reside,
Crafting soft whispers, with hearts open wide.
Ideas take flight on the wings of a dream,
In the workshop of whispers, nothing's as it seems.

Hands stained with colors, a canvas so bare,
Each stroke of our voices, a bond we repair.
With laughter that dances, and insights that spark,
We forge through the shadows, igniting the dark.

Paper and pencil, our tools of the trade,
Together we sculpt, with faith unafraid.
In the warmth of this space, our spirits ignite,
A glorious union, as day turns to night.

The whispers grow louder, gaining in trust,
Turning to dreams, as we map out our thirst.
Creating a future, where visions entwine,
In the workshop of whispers, our souls brightly shine.

## Crafting Companionship

With time as our fabric, we weave our threads,
Through laughter and sorrow, where no one dreads.
In moments of stillness, we see each embrace,
Crafting companionship, in this sacred space.

Side by side we gather, intent in our gaze,
Counting the blessings, in myriad ways.
As seasons of life change, our bond stays true,
In the tapestry woven, it's me and it's you.

From shared whispered secrets to bold, joyful cries,
In the heart of togetherness, our spirit lies.
Building foundations, both sturdy and strong,
Crafting companionship; we always belong.

Through storms that may come, we weather the fight,
Together we shine, like stars in the night.
In every adventure, in every new plan,
We find in one another, the strength to expand.

## **The Lab of Emotional Growth**

In the lab of emotions, we gather and learn,
With hearts like petals, in sunlight they burn.
Experimenting with hopes, we grow ever wise,
In the garden of feelings, our spirits arise.

Through valleys of sorrow and peaks filled with glee,
We cultivate patience and let our hearts see.
With kindness as soil, and love as the sun,
In the lab of growth, we flourish as one.

Each moment a lesson, every tear a release,
As we plant the seeds, we nurture in peace.
In the chemistry of care, we find our own way,
Transforming our fears into hope every day.

With open minds gathered, we build and explore,
In the lab of emotions, there's always much more.
As we chart our own paths, together we thrive,
In the whispers of growth, our spirits alive.

## The Textbook of Togetherness

In the library of hearts, we find our way,
Page by page, we learn to stay.
With every chapter, our bond will grow,
The ink of friendship in every flow.

When storms arise, together we stand,
Hand in hand, we'll understand.
Each lesson learned, a thread we weave,
In the fabric of life, we believe.

In silence shared, in laughter bright,
In darkest hours, we bring the light.
We write our stories, side by side,
In this textbook, love is our guide.

Through trials faced, through joy's embrace,
Together we find our rightful place.
Every moment penned, every sigh,
In the textbook of together, you and I.

So let us keep turning each precious page,
With every year, we'll grow in age.
In the margins, our dreams will stay,
Together forever, come what may.

## **Harvesting the Fruits of Devotion**

In the garden of trust, we plant the seeds,
With love as our soil, we nurture needs.
Under the sun, our spirits bloom,
Harvesting joy, dispelling gloom.

Through seasons of change, together we toil,
Rooting deep within this rich soil.
Gathering blessings, one by one,
The fruits of our labor, sweet as the sun.

In every vine, our dreams entwine,
With hearts committed, we'll shine and shine.
The bounty we share, a feast divine,
In unity's warmth, our souls align.

As the harvest comes, we gather near,
With thankful hearts, we shed our fear.
A table set for all to see,
The fruits of devotion, you and me.

So let us savor the sweet embrace,
In this garden, we've found our place.
With every bite, our love will grow,
In the harvest of life, together we sow.

## Prototype of Heartstrings

In the workshop of dreams, we craft our fate,
Heartstrings entwined, we resonate.
With every vibration, our souls connect,
Prototype of love, we'll perfect.

With careful hands, we shape the mold,
Each moment shared, a story told.
Through trials and errors, we learn to bend,
The art of loving, with no end.

In sketches drawn, our visions align,
In the blueprint of life, your hand in mine.
Each heartstring pulled, a melody sweet,
In this symphony, we feel complete.

As we build our world, piece by piece,
In shared laughter, we find our peace.
With every heartbeat, our rhythm grows,
In this prototype, our love overflows.

So let us refine this magnificent plan,
In the workshop of life, you hold my hand.
Together we stand, no dreams apart,
In the prototype of our loving hearts.

## The Manual of Mutual Understanding

In the pages of wisdom, we seek to learn,
With open minds, our hearts will turn.
Every conflict faced, a lesson gained,
In the manual of us, love is retained.

With every chapter, we closely read,
Finding the means to meet each need.
Through gentle words and listening ears,
In mutual understanding, we conquer fears.

As we navigate through twists and bends,
With patience fostered, we make amends.
In every dialogue, our truth displayed,
In this manual, our love is laid.

With every turn, new insights bloom,
In the garden of thought, we make room.
For every viewpoint, we create a space,
In the manual of us, we find our grace.

So let's keep learning, with hearts so wide,
In the manual of love, you're by my side.
Every word written, a bridge to span,
In understanding's realm, together we stand.

## Alchemy of Souls

In whispers soft, the secrets weave,
Of hearts entwined, and dreams believe.
The night ignites with sparks of fate,
A dance of souls, so intricate.

Among the stars, our stories blend,
With every sigh, a message send.
The alchemy of time and space,
Transforms our lives, a warm embrace.

Through trials faced, we learn to fly,
In depths of love, we touch the sky.
With open hearts, we craft our art,
A bond that's forged, we'll never part.

Eternal light within us glows,
The magic grows, as fortune sows.
With every heartbeat, truth unfolds,
In alchemy of souls, we hold.

So let us chase the fleeting hours,
In realms of dreams, where hope empowers.
Together we shall brave the night,
With souls aligned, in endless flight.

## Shadows and Sunlight

In silent corners, shadows play,
While golden beams keep dark at bay.
Each moment caught in light's embrace,
Dances with shadows, finds its place.

The twilight speaks in hues of gray,
As day surrenders to the fray.
The sun dips low, the night awakes,
In whispered dreams, the silence breaks.

Yet in this blend of dark and bright,
A beauty shines, ignites the night.
For every shadow cast with care,
There blooms a flower, rich and rare.

As moonlit paths reflect our thoughts,
In every heart, a battle fought.
With courage found in beams of light,
We navigate through darkest plight.

So let us dance on lines we draw,
In shades of truth and nature's law.
Embrace the blend, both dark and bright,
For life's a canvas, pure delight.

## The Language of Longing

In every glance, unspoken sighs,
Hearts communicate beneath the skies.
A yearning deep, with words unsaid,
In silence, love's true voice is fed.

The distance calls, the stars align,
With every heartbeat, paths entwine.
Longing whispers soft and clear,
An echo felt, when you are near.

In twilight's glow, a secret shared,
With dreams and hopes, our souls laid bare.
The language flows from heart to heart,
In depths of love, we never part.

A single touch, a fleeting glance,
Ignites the fire, begins the dance.
With every breath, the world expands,
In love's embrace, we take our stand.

So let us speak in silence true,
Where every heartbeat sings of you.
In every moment, rich and strong,
We find our peace in longing's song.

## **Heartbeats and Hypotheses**

In rhythm's pulse, our theories rise,
With every beat, the truth defies.
We ponder life in fleeting frames,
As passions spark and fate reclaims.

Through questions asked, our minds explore,
The universe holds keys to more.
In heartbeats strong, we seek to know,
The paths of love that ebb and flow.

With every sigh, a world unfurls,
Hypotheses in gentle swirls.
We map the stars, unravel fate,
In every touch, we navigate.

From whispers shared, new questions form,
In heart's embrace, we feel the warm.
Theories built on hopes and dreams,
In life's great dance, nothing's as seems.

So let us chase the pulse of time,
In leaps of faith, our spirits climb.
For in each heartbeat, truths collide,
In love's embrace, we boldly stride.

## The Framework of Forever

In shadows deep, we find our way,
Beneath the stars, our dreams at play.
Each moment's thread we tightly weave,
In heart's embrace, we dare believe.

A tapestry of hopes untold,
In whispered secrets, we grow bold.
With every step, we chase the light,
Our love a beacon, shining bright.

Through storms that rage and winds that howl,
Our bond, a steadfast, sacred vow.
In silence shared, we hear the call,
Together we rise, together we fall.

The past a guide, the future vast,
In moments fleeting, forever cast.
With hands entwined, we face the day,
In the framework of forever, we'll stay.

As seasons shift and time holds its breath,
In every ending, there's life in death.
Through dawns and dusks, we journey on,
In love's embrace, we're never gone.

## The Labyrinth of Longing

In corridors of deep desire,
We walk the paths, hearts full of fire.
Each turn conceals a hidden dream,
In this maze of longing, we gleam.

With every sigh, a spark ignites,
Navigating through starry nights.
Past echoes whisper secrets old,
In shadows, our stories unfold.

Through twisted hallways, we explore,
The depths of yearnings we can't ignore.
Each step a dance, each glance a plea,
In this labyrinth, set our souls free.

Hopes entwined like ivy on stone,
In solitude, we find our own.
Yet through the maze, we seek a guide,
In every longing, love won't hide.

So hand in hand, we'll chart the course,
With every heartbeat, feel the force.
In this labyrinth, we'll find our song,
In the dance of longing, we belong.

## Revelations in Reflection

In still waters, truths emerge,
As we dive deep, our hearts converge.
Each ripple speaks of tales untold,
In reflective gleams, we break the mold.

Like mirrors casting back our fears,
We learn to soften, face the years.
The whispers of the past resound,
In quiet moments, wisdom found.

With each reflection, a brighter hue,
Revealing shades of me and you.
In clarity of soul laid bare,
We'll find the strength to truly dare.

As dawn awakens thought anew,
In reflections, we seek what's true.
The edges soften, love takes flight,
In revelations, we find the light.

So let the waters guide our way,
Through depths unknown, we'll not sway.
In mirrored dreams, our spirits blend,
In reflections found, our hearts transcend.

## Testing the Waters of Togetherness

In gentle waves, we dip our toes,
Exploring places where love grows.
With every splash, we share a grin,
In this adventure, let us begin.

The currents pull, a thrilling ride,
Together we face the rising tide.
With buoyant hearts, we'll sail away,
In waters deep, our spirits play.

Vows written in the salt and sand,
A promise made, a touch of hand.
Each wave a chance to start anew,
In this vast ocean, me and you.

As storms may brew and skies may grey,
We'll hold each other, come what may.
For in the depths, we find our peace,
Testing the waters, love won't cease.

So let us dive into the blue,
With hearts as one and dreams in view.
In togetherness, we find our place,
In the waters' embrace, we'll leave our trace.

## Schematics of Shared Secrets

In whispers soft, our secrets lie,
Drawn in ink beneath the sky.
Each line a trust, a gentle thread,
Binding hearts where words are spread.

Maps of dreams, we sketch by night,
Outlining hopes in shared delight.
In silence shared, we understand,
A bond created, hand in hand.

With every truth, a layer peels,
Unraveling thoughts, what love reveals.
The schematics of hearts entwined,
In every secret, our souls aligned.

A blueprint drawn, two lives designed,
With laughter and tears, our ties confined.
The beauty lies in what we share,
Making sure that hearts are bare.

So hold these secrets, dear and tight,
In shadows deep, the stars ignite.
For in the dark, our stories gleam,
A tapestry woven from shared dream.

## The Potion of Passion

In twilight's glow, our hearts ignite,
With whispered spells, the world feels right.
A potion brewed from laughter's sound,
In every drop, our love is found.

With every glance, the magic grows,
A liquid fire where desire flows.
Stirred by hands that long to touch,
In this concoction, we are so much.

The recipe calls for trust and care,
A hint of longing in vibrant air.
With each heartbeat, the potion stirs,
In passion's dance, our spirits blur.

So sip this blend, let moments reign,
In every taste, forget the pain.
For in this cup lies vibrant life,
A potion shared by you and I.

Together we become the brew,
In twilight's haze, our love feels true.
As stars align, we sip the night,
A potion of passion, pure delight.

## **Building Bonds Within**

Brick by brick, we start to build,
A fortress strong, our hearts fulfilled.
With laughter framing every wall,
In tears, we find a way to call.

Foundations laid on trust and care,
Each moment shared, a breath of air.
We pencil dreams in spaces wide,
Constructing joy, a rising tide.

Windows open to the skies above,
Letting in the light of love.
Together, we design the way,
Each bond we form, a brighter day.

Through storms that shake, we stand our ground,
In unity, our strength is found.
With open hearts, we dare to soar,
Building bonds, forevermore.

So come, my friend, let's carve our names,
In every brick, ignite the flames.
For in this journey, side by side,
We'll find a home in love and pride.

## The Anatomy of Affection

In gentle touches, love takes form,
Anatomy of hearts, the perfect norm.
With every smile, a spark ignites,
Healing wounds, in soft delights.

Emotions rise like waves of tide,
Carrying us on love's wild ride.
Fingers trace the lines of fate,
In affection's grasp, we resonate.

Each heartbeat sings a tender song,
In this embrace where we belong.
Structuring love with trust and care,
Building a bond that's rich and rare.

Through every glance, we understand,
The anatomy of hearts so grand.
With every laugh, our spirits swirl,
A love unwrapped, a shining pearl.

So come, dear heart, let's celebrate,
The precious ties we cultivate.
In every moment, let love reflect,
The anatomy of deepest affection.

## The Tapestry of Togetherness

In a world spun from threads of light,
We weave our dreams, our hopes in flight.
Each moment stitched, a bond so tight,
Together we stand, through day and night.

With colors bright, our stories blend,
In laughter shared, our spirits mend.
Hand in hand, our hearts transcend,
A tapestry of love, no end.

Through storms we face, our courage bold,
In whispered words, our truths unfold.
A symphony in hearts retold,
A legacy of warmth and gold.

As seasons change, our threads may fray,
Yet still we choose to find our way.
In every stitch, a promise lay,
A masterpiece, come what may.

So let us dance, in joy and grace,
With every step, we find our place.
Together woven, time can't erase,
In love, forever, we embrace.

## Elements of Euphoria

Beneath the sky, where dreams take flight,
In whispered winds, we chase the light.
With every laugh, a spark ignites,
Elements merge in pure delight.

The sun, it warms our eager souls,
While moonlit nights create the whole.
In gentle waves, the ocean rolls,
Euphoria, in nature's bowls.

As raindrops dance on thirsty earth,
They sing of life, of joy, of birth.
In every heartbeat, find our worth,
In passion's fire, we find our mirth.

With stars above, we dream and roam,
In unity, we find our home.
Through every trial, we'll not condone,
The thrill of life, we claim our own.

Together we rise, like dawn's first glow,
In harmony, our spirits flow.
Each moment shared, a chance to grow,
Euphoria's song forever sow.

## The Heart's Experiment

In silence deep, our hearts unfold,
With secrets shared, a truth retold.
Together we dare, to be so bold,
The heart's experiment, love's gold.

Through trust and pain, we learn to feel,
Each tender gaze, a fragile seal.
In every heartbeat, we reveal,
The way we shape our fate, ideal.

Like chemists blend their finest art,
We mix our thoughts, ignite the spark.
In whispered dreams, we play our part,
The heart's experiment, a beating heart.

Through trial and error, joy and fears,
We learn to sift through hopes and tears.
In every laugh, a bond appears,
The heart's experiment, for years.

So let us gather, hand in hand,
With every step, we understand.
In love's vast sea, we'll gently stand,
The heart's experiment, so grand.

## The Seeds of Affection

In quiet soil, our love takes root,
A fragile sprout, with tender shoot.
With care and time, we nurture fruit,
The seeds of affection, absolute.

Through sunlit days and storms we brave,
In kindness shared, the hearts we save.
Each gentle touch, a bond we pave,
The seeds of affection, bold and brave.

As seasons change, our love will grow,
In every word, the truth will show.
In shadows cast, our spirits glow,
The seeds of affection, ever slow.

Through laughter's song and quiet nights,
In each embrace, we feel the heights.
Together woven, life's delights,
The seeds of affection, pure as sights.

So let us stand, hand in hand,
In fields of love, together planned.
In every heart, a promise grand,
The seeds of affection, life's demand.

# **Reflections in the Mirror of Us**

In the glass, our truths collide,
Shadows dance and secrets bide.
Each glance an echo, soft and clear,
Whispers of love and hints of fear.

Time unveils the layers deep,
Memories cherished, promises we keep.
In every smile, a tale unfolds,
The warmth of our hearts, like embers, holds.

Through the mirror, we see our flaws,
Yet in acceptance, our beauty draws.
With every scar, we learn to thrive,
In the reflection, our souls come alive.

Together we stand, unyielding and bold,
In the mirror of us, a story told.
Each moment crafted, a work of art,
Unified visions, a seamless heart.

With every gaze, we redefine,
The love we share, the bond we entwine.
Through the glass, we choose to see,
The reflections of you, the reflections of me.

## **Experiments in Trust**

In the balance, we tread so light,
Testing waters, day and night.
A leap of faith, hand in hand,
Building bridges, where dreams stand.

Every word a tentative thread,
Woven closer, where hopes are fed.
With every tear, a lesson sought,
In the fragility, we learn what's taught.

Trust is fragile, yet it grows,
With every challenge, the bond shows.
In the silence, we find our way,
Through experiments, love's dance in play.

With each failure, we rise anew,
In the journey, the spark shines through.
Investigating the depths we find,
In trust's embrace, two hearts aligned.

Together we mold the clay of chance,
In every twist, a newfound dance.
With fragile steps, we forge our fate,
Through trust's experiments, we find our state.

## **Blossoms of Understanding**

In the garden of hearts, we sow,
Seeds of empathy, watch them grow.
Petals unfurl with each shared tale,
In the soft sunlight, love prevails.

Through dialogue's rain, we nurture the roots,
In the soil of kindness, understanding shoots.
With every conflict, a chance to mend,
In the blooms, we find, our hearts extend.

Colorful whispers of varied hues,
Painting our visions, blending our views.
With every petal, a voice is heard,
In the silence, we share a word.

Among the thorns, we bravely tread,
In the blooms of wisdom, our souls are wed.
Compassion's fragrance fills the air,
In blossoms of understanding, we find repair.

Together we flourish, in sunlight's embrace,
In the garden of love, we find our place.
Through the seasons, we nurture with care,
In the blooms of life, love's truth we share.

## The Canvas of Companionship

Upon this canvas, colors blend,
Strokes of laughter, where hearts mend.
Each hue a memory, vivid and bright,
In the art of love, we find our light.

With every brush, a moment's muse,
In the layers of life, we choose to use.
Shades of sorrow, dips of glee,
Crafting a picture, just you and me.

Together we paint, with whispers soft,
In the dance of time, we rise aloft.
Each moment captured, a tale to share,
In the canvas of companionship, we lay bare.

From bold hues of joy to subtle shades,
In the gallery of life, our love cascades.
Through every stroke, our spirits soar,
On this canvas, we're forevermore.

With every glance, the portrait glows,
In the beauty of us, love overflows.
Together we create, side by side,
In the canvas of companionship, we abide.

## **Threads of Connection**

In the quiet whispers of the night,
We find the bonds that feel just right.
Each word a thread, each glance a seam,
We weave the fabric of a dream.

Through laughter shared and tears combined,
Our hearts embrace, our souls aligned.
A tapestry of moments spun,
In every thread, we are as one.

With every touch, with every sigh,
The world expands, we learn to fly.
The ties that bind us, delicate yet strong,
Together, we create our song.

In the ebb and flow, the give and take,
We navigate the paths we make.
Each twist and turn, a step we share,
In this vast dance, we find our care.

As light cascades through shadows cast,
We hold each moment, make it last.
In every heartbeat, every choice,
Together we're stronger, we find our voice.

## **The Journey of Hearts Entwined**

Two souls embarking on a path,
Through joy and sorrow, love's sweet wrath.
With every stumble, we learn to rise,
In the gaze of trust, a thousand skies.

Hand in hand, we navigate the bends,
With every heartbeat, the journey mends.
In whispers shared and stories told,
We find a warmth that won't grow cold.

Through storms that test, we hold our ground,
In the chaos, a love profound.
With every challenge, we find our way,
Each step together, come what may.

On this road of dreams and fears,
We celebrate both laughter and tears.
A journey painted with shades of grace,
In each other, we find our place.

As time unfolds, we grow, we bloom,
In every shadow, we cast away gloom.
Two hearts entwined in a dance divine,
The journey continues, forever mine.

## Variables in Vulnerability

In the cracks of armor, light seeps through,
Embracing weakness, we find what's true.
Each scar a story, each crack a tale,
In vulnerability, we learn to sail.

The heart laid bare, the mind exposed,
In honesty's gaze, our fears are closed.
With every tear, we shed the weight,
In the openness, we find our fate.

Like shifting sands beneath our feet,
We learn to dance to love's heartbeat.
In the chaos, we discover peace,
In the rawness, our fears release.

For every risk, there's beauty gained,
In tender moments, love unchained.
In the variables of our embrace,
We find the strength to face the space.

With every glance and every sigh,
In vulnerability, we learn to fly.
The brave hearts open, the fearless thrive,
In the depths of truth, we come alive.

## The Labyrinth of Emotion

In the maze where feelings swirl and weave,
We navigate the paths we believe.
Each turn a question, each wall a fear,
In the heart's labyrinth, we draw near.

Twists of joy and corners of pain,
Through the shadows, we dance in the rain.
With every heartbeat, a riddle to solve,
In the depths of the maze, we evolve.

A symphony played on the strings of the heart,
In the chaos of feelings, we're set apart.
Through tangled emotions, we find the sound,
In the labyrinth's embrace, love is found.

In moments of silence, clarity speaks,
In the folds of the labyrinth, hope peaks.
With every step, we learn and grow,
In the journey of emotion, we let love flow.

Through the twists and turns, joy and despair,
We find strength in the love that we share.
In the labyrinth of feeling, we seek the light,
Together we wander, united, ignited.

## Tinkering with Trust

In the workshop of our minds,
We carve the shapes of belief,
With hands both gentle and firm,
We build bridges of relief.

Each promise a tool in hand,
Each whisper a blueprint clear,
We mix our hopes like paint,
Creating trust without fear.

But cracks can form in silence,
When doubt begins to roll,
We patch them with kind words,
Offering the heart's console.

Curate the fragile fragments,
A careful design to uphold,
Tinkering takes patience,
In the warmth of stories told.

So in this craft of love,
Let's find the strength to adapt,
With every chance we take,
We weave trust, tightly wrapped.

## The Experiment of Empathy

In the lab of human hearts,
We mix a potion of care,
With kindness as our catalyst,
We breathe in the shared air.

Through lenses made of laughter,
We observe life's subtle shifts,
Collecting stories like samples,
In the tapestry of gifts.

When a tear slips quietly,
We note the weight it bears,
Our findings grow in silence,
As love erases despair.

Each moment a hypothesis,
Exploration of the soul,
In every act of compassion,
We find the pieces whole.

Let's document our findings,
In the journal of our days,
For every heart we connect,
Transforms the world in small ways.

## Insights from the Heart Chamber

Deep within our heart chamber,
Resides a treasure trove,
Each beat a whispered secret,
Of dreams we seek to prove.

With echoes of our adventures,
And lessons sewn in time,
We find wisdom in still moments,
In the rhythm and the rhyme.

As shadows dance around us,
Illuminating our plight,
We grasp the hidden knowledge,
In the depths of twilight.

Each connection sparks a whisper,
A flicker of shared light,
Through trials and tribulations,
We find our path in night.

So, listen to your heart songs,
Let them guide your way home,
For in each note of longing,
We'll never be alone.

## **The Palette of Passionate Colors**

In the artist's vibrant studio,
Colors splash and dance,
With every stroke of passion,
We give our hearts a chance.

Red sings of fierce emotions,
Blue whispers dreams untold,
Yellow beams like summer sun,
As stories start to unfold.

With green, we find our balance,
A calming hue of peace,
While purples speak of magic,
Where our fears find release.

Each shade a part of living,
A memoir in its hue,
We blend our hopes with heartbeats,
Creating something new.

So, let's create a canvas,
With strokes both bold and fine,
In the palette of our passions,
Our lives will intertwine.

Milton Keynes UK
Ingram Content Group UK Ltd.
UKHW022049111124
451035UK00014B/1024

9 789916 866245